Conflict resolution for beginners

Resolving conflicts in everyday life, in relationships and at work

How to recognize conflict potential and resolve conflicts in a goal-oriented manner

Matthias Ernst

CONTENTS

Conflict resolution in everyday life

WHAT YOU CAN EXPECT IN THIS BOOK

Whether in everyday life or at work - wherever people and different characters meet, there is potential for conflict. Do you often find yourself in situations where minor disputes lead to lengthy arguments or where you fail to assert your interests? Do you perhaps jeopardize relationships with people who are important to you or with whom you are dependent? Do you perhaps even feel less educated or eloquent than your counterpart after discussions? You don't have to. This book will help you to resolve such interpersonal disagreements, arguments and discussions quickly and easily so that you can assert your point of view in a moderate manner without causing lasting damage to your relationships with others. It is perfectly natural to get into these situations and, as we have all experienced, they can quickly become heated and emotionally charged. This is not your fault. However, it is possible to avoid this in a few simple steps and still come out of the conflict satisfied and confident.

On the following pages, you will be introduced to the problem and informed about current research in the field of conflict resolution, which will be illustrated using realistic examples. You will then be given a summary of what you can take away from this, before finally being given a brief, easy-to-remember guide that you can use to achieve positive results in your everyday life.

WHY CONFLICT RESOLUTION IS SO IMPORTANT

Every time you get into a conflict, you miss an opportunity to gain added value from the conversation. Because even a conversation that is irrelevant to you at least has the benefit of entertaining you. You can learn a lesson, gain new knowledge or alternative perspectives from most conversations. It is also possible to learn something about yourself, practise argumentation, clear up your own misconceptions, prejudices or gaps in your education. In some conflicts, even relationships, business deals or finances are at stake. However, you miss out on all of this as soon as you plunge into a conflict and fail to resolve it.

It is also clear that not every conflict can be avoided, and it would be the wrong approach to always avoid them because you would have no added value. It is therefore essential to find ways to resolve conflicts and reap the potential added value. However, mere willpower and assertiveness are not enough. In the long term, stubbornly insisting on every dispute and sitting it out until the other person gives in can be just as damaging as always giving in yourself. This could damage relationships in the long term and put you offside. Finding this middle ground between de-escalation and purposefulness will help you in the long term in all areas of life. You will be able to walk away from any heated situation with the desired outcome and all parties will feel good about it. This makes conflict resolution a core skill in social interaction.

UNDERSTANDING THE PROBLEM

In order to understand how to resolve a conflict, it helps to first understand how often banal and calm conversations can develop into heated arguments in the first place. All you have to do is look at your own behavior. People tend to be convinced of their points of view and not question them without cause. So it can often be unimaginable, downright frustrating, when someone else has a different opinion. This person is most likely just as convinced of his or her own views and hardened fronts form. If a discussion then becomes personal, emotions can often no longer be averted. In addition, pride and stubbornness may prevent the disputants from moving away from their points of view. Previous dislikes towards the other party can also lead to people being prejudiced and negative towards the other person's opinion.

Finally, volume also plays a role, which spirals in the situations mentioned and distracts more and more from the actual topic. As you can see, it doesn't take much to lay the foundation for an argument. The topic can be anything from preferences to the sports team to politics and business to salary negotiations at work.

You can apply what you have learned here universally to any topic.

The first thing to note is that the origin of conflicts usually lies in one's own subjectivity, which prevents one from taking a sober view of the situation. The more heated the dispute, the less rational the players are. This creates a vicious circle that can lead to great potential for conflict in all kinds of conversations. As soon as the focus is less on the actual subject matter and more on the person behind it, an argument is almost inevitable. In everyday life, you will be able to recognize this pattern in discussions about your favourite sports team or the like, for example, because people are already subjective at the beginning of the conversation due to sympathies. In professional life, this can be seen, for example, in critical discussions with superiors. When confronted with our own shortcomings, we tend to automatically adopt a defensive stance, become less receptive and reject any criticism, even if it is justified. This not only prevents a healthy culture of discussion, but also a good opportunity to reflect and possibly even eradicate mistakes.

However, this guide does not necessarily help you to avoid conflict - even if the methods developed here can certainly be similarly helpful in this area. This guide will show you how it is possible to resolve a conflict that has already arisen without any losses. So you are in an intense discussion, have been arguing with your work colleague for weeks or simply cannot convince your boss to give you a pay rise. Things have already been said that have affected the other person personally and you have already invested so much in persuading the other person that you no longer want to back down. The sides are deadlocked. This is the crux of the problem: how do I resolve a situation like this? You don't want to lose face and ideally you also want the result you are hoping for. But your counterpart is pursuing the same goal. Pride, subjectivity, frustration and antipathy on the part of the participants have exactly the opposite effect.

If it continues like this, the conflict escalates and both lose more than was originally at stake. A situation from which both can benefit, such as a conversation to pass the time, quickly becomes one from which both suffer. Comparisons can be drawn here with a game of poker.

You have to weigh up whether to give up your bet and lose, but still hold on to your remaining chips, or whether to go all-in and then win or lose everything. The parallels end there, however, because it is not at all helpful to approach human interaction like a game of cards and tricks. However, the poker comparison makes the tricky situation clear. So how can this con-flict be resolved?

CONCEPTS FOR PROBLEM SOLVING

To answer this, this guide will first approach the situation from an abstract perspective and explain the theories and methods to you, before applying them concretely and vividly in real life, just as you will be able to do after reading this book. But first back to the problems that need to be overcome: there is a conflict of interest between both parties, there is emotionality at play, which prevents an objective view of the situation and causes the situation to only get worse.

On the other side are the goals. What is your desired end result of the conflict? You most likely want to get along with your disputing partner, but often also want to get what you started arguing about in the first place - whether it's a pay rise, a favor or something else. In disputes, you are more interested in not looking stupid and being in the right, possibly also in convincing the other person. In order to reconcile these interests - harmony and profit for you - there is a solution that is often considered utopian: the win-win situation. Both parties come out of the conflict as winners. In the course of this book, however, you will discover that this is possible more often than you might initially think.

The Harvard concept

The so-called Harvard concept is also based on this idea. This is an internationally proven method of conflict resolution that is primarily used in legal disputes to avoid a dispute in court. It was developed by Roger Fisher and William Ury in 1981, who took inspiration from the Harvard Negotiation Project at Harvard University, hence the name. It is based on simple solutions that can be applied regardless of the dispute in a professional context and attempts to ensure that the disputing parties can both benefit from the dispute in 5 steps.

First of all, the structure of this method should be explained and you will already notice that the problems and causes of conflict that were previously worked out are reflected and that these are specifically counteracted. The first point of the Harvard concept is: "Separate the person from the problem!". This means that you should avoid projecting your feelings about a problem or issue onto the person behind it. It makes no sense and is even less beneficial to demonize your conflict partner for their beliefs and interests.

Instead of allowing these to merge, it is much more advisable to take a sober look at the situation and initially leave the person responsible for it out of the equation. It doesn't matter how naive, small-minded or narrow-minded the person acts and thinks or how much they are to blame for the conflict. All of this should be disregarded for the time being. So don't focus on the person themselves, but on what they are saying and pursuing; don't try to point out character flaws, but look for solutions to the problem. But even then, it is advisable to do this calmly and considerately, otherwise the person behind the persuasion may feel attacked despite everything.

You may find this difficult at first and, admittedly, it often goes against human intuition, but it will help you to take unnecessary heat out of the situation early on. Because that is also the aim of this first step: de-escalation. You may not have come any closer to a substantive solution to the problem, but it nevertheless lays the necessary foundation for a factual solution. After all, what is the point of having found a solution on a substantive level a long time ago if you have upset the other person so much that they no longer listen to you and are only prepared to drive you both deeper into the conflict? This is why we want to introduce or bring back a healthy culture of discussion in which no one involved has to feel attacked.

This slows down the situation and takes away the emotionality. Many conflicts escalate precisely when the parties feel personally attacked. You may have already noticed that this helps to counter the above-mentioned problems of personal dislikes, stubbornness and pride and makes it possible to approach the content rationally in the subsequent steps.

So what does this mean in concrete terms? This can be better understood using an example. You are in a dispute with your colleague with whom you are working on a project. He is completely averse to technology and therefore insists on giving the final presentation orally in front of handwritten posters. You, on the other hand, are competent when it comes to PowerPoint presentations and know for sure that you could convey the project much more vividly this way. Your colleague mocks you for this view. So now separate the view from the person. It is completely understandable to hold a grudge against your colleague, and this is where the first step comes in.

Don't blame your colleague for the conflict and don't draw conclusions about their character from their views. Approach the situation soberly. This first step largely takes place in your head; no criticism of the view that a handwritten presentation is better should become criticism of your colleague.

Your colleague is not old-fashioned and stubbornly closed to technology, he just has what you consider to be an old-fashioned view in this specific conflict. The problem is not one of generations or attitudes, but simply a question of how you can best give your presentation. There is simply no point in trying to convert your counterpart at this point, so look at the problem and not your colleague.

The second point of the Harvard concept goes in a similar direction. It recommends focusing on interests rather than positions. What does your opponent actually want? What do you actually want? How can you meet this interest? Are your interests and his compatible? You should ask yourself these questions and not dwell on his convictions. So look to the future and look constructively for ways out of the conflict instead of dwelling on present or even past statements.

At the same time, there is no point in constantly emphasizing one's own positions; instead, it is far more helpful to show the intention behind them and explain what the goal is. In the end, skirmishes on an ideological level are skipped and the focus is placed directly on where the convictions are reflected, and only to the extent that interests conflict, so that unnecessary debates about right and wrong are avoided.

The intention behind this is similar to that of the first point: it only provides avoidable potential for conflict to dwell on positions for longer, so the aim is to de-escalate again. Beliefs are often firmly rooted in one's own personality, so criticism of beliefs can be perceived as criticism of one's own personality. However, it is not only emotionality that is avoided in this way. It is simply more time-efficient to observe the part of the conviction that also affects the other person. After all, interest is based on conviction and only that is relevant for a conflict in this area. This future-oriented perspective brings the parties closer together, bridges differences and seeks a solution based on what both parties want, not what they think.

Now for another example. You and an employee have the task of providing transportation for the workforce with an allocated budget. Your colleague cares about the environment, so he suggests paying for annual train tickets. You, on the other hand, are a car enthusiast, categorically reject train travel and think it would be best to use the money to buy four cars that your colleagues can use freely. The potential for conflict is not far away here, given that you both have such opposing views. The wrong approach would therefore be to argue about whether cars are an environmental sin or not, or about whether train travel is inadequate for commuting. Focus on the interest at hand and also look to the future in search of solutions. Your colleague's interest is to offer train tickets, you want to offer cars.

This should be treated abstractly and has nothing to do with ideologies regarding climate protection. Don't ask "How do I convince my employee that climate protection by train is the wrong way to go?", but ask "How do I convince him that the budget would be better invested in cars, or is there possibly even a way to satisfy both interests?". What if, for example, the employees could decide or the budget could be shared? Are electric cars an option? In this way, there is no fundamental discussion and constructive consideration can be given to the future of your budget, with both sides pulling in the same direction.

The Harvard concept continues with the third step: find different solutions and look for ones that benefit both parties. Where previously the focus was on a healthy basis, creativity is now required to find an objective solution. The aim is to find as many ways out of the conflict as possible. Of course, the focus here is not just on quantity. The greater the mutual benefit, the better the approach to conflict resolution.

The quickest way to develop these is to let your creativity run free and record all the ideas that seem possible. It helps to always keep both interests equally in mind, because as soon as your partner benefits, you benefit from the fact that they are more cooperative and more willing to compromise. So find the other person's interests, what is most important to them, and look for ways to offer them something of value to them, while you yourself can also make a profit.

This step lies at the heart of the Harvard concept. It is based on the idea that conflict should not be seen as something disruptive, but rather as an opportunity for new cooperation and joint development. The intention is for both parties to emerge as winners, which would generally mean that there is no longer any potential for conflict. With regard to the scope of application of the Harvard concept in contractual disputes under private international law, one variant for mutual gain stands out in particular: cake enlargement. In these disputes, this means that instead of bringing a monetary claim, both parties - often companies - agree to receive shares from each other, to make a profit by working together or to create value in some other way that benefits them both in the long term. This can be investments in joint projects or support from other companies that help both parties.

It is not a prerequisite that the solution to the problem concerns the problem, it is more about satisfaction through mutual help, so that ultimately the gain through cooperation is greater than the loss through conflict. Even beyond this rather elusive world, the idea can be applied to individuals. The idea behind the Harvard method requires the aforementioned level of creativity, but can open doors and close partnerships. Because the parties to the conflict suffer from the same problem, solving it can also benefit both of them. From this perspective, the opposing parties are therefore in the same boat.

Imagine that your company owes another company, which you supply on a long-term basis, a new delivery of a certain product due to a mistake made by the producer who in turn supplied you. The other company desperately wants these goods, but you think that you are not responsible for the mistakes made by your producer, who is unreliable anyway, which is why you are annoyed. You also need payment for the order as your company is in a financial bottleneck. Keep reminding yourself that you are in the same boat here. Then look freely for possible solutions, there are no wrong ideas. Your business partner wants goods, you don't want to lose money. Even if these interests seem incompatible at first glance, try to find ways in which you can both benefit from each other.

For example, you could suggest that your contractual partner invests the necessary payment in another, more reliable producer for you so that they can now supply you. This could eliminate the delivery problems, which is good for both of you. Now you could supply your partner better and in larger quantities, he receives the goods on time and without defects, so he pays sooner. This would benefit both sides in the long term. You could also add a free portion of goods to the next delivery as a further incentive. This would preserve the relationship, the working relationship would work better in the long term and both parties would benefit financially. Of course, this would only be one of many options, but the idea is clear. Try to offer your conflict opponent something that appeals to them and look for ways to benefit from it, because cooperation always offers more advantages than conflict.

Point four of the Harvard method offers assessment criteria for the solution. According to this, the situation and possible solutions should only be evaluated based on objective criteria. Personal preferences, prejudices or fears must be left out of the equation. The criteria should be objectively measurable, i.e. in such a way that both parties come to the same conclusion without any leeway.

Figures, data and, under certain circumstances, statistics are ideal for this, although these can also be interpreted differently depending on the intention. Comparative cases can also help you to better foresee consequences and categorize scenarios. Use these pillars to determine whether a solution idea is suitable for both sides.

The aim of this point is to remove subjectivity from the conflict. As mentioned above, everyone has biases with regard to their own way of thinking, they are convinced of themselves. However, this is only possible if both ways of thinking are assessed based on different criteria. If they are assessed on the basis of objective criteria that both sides can agree on, it is easier to determine what the interests of the other party entail and what the best solution is. In this way, the decision is based on facts, not emotions.

You are now in the following scenario: You and a colleague are on the architecture team for the new company building. You have a difference of opinion regarding the color of the office rooms. Your colleague wants the rooms painted dark blue, you prefer white and hate the color blue. So it's up to you to find the criteria to resolve this dispute.

The fact that you have a personal aversion to the color blue should not be a criterion. Nor would you want your employee's preferences to determine the office color. So look for objective criteria. First of all, the financial aspect is always a good place to start. How much do the colors cost? Are there differences? Get quotes and you have a fair criterion. What other facts could there be about office paint colors?

This question may seem trivial, but if you look into it, you might find other criteria. How does the color affect the light and brightness of the room? Are both desired colors readily available or are there waiting times? Finally, scientific findings can help. However, you should take this with a grain of salt and make sure that the results are unanimous and that you are not citing a single study that supports your interest. In this case, there are countless elaborate and unanimous studies on the effect of room colors on people. Cite this and you have another point of reference. This approach ensures that both sides are on the same page and can discuss from the same perspective.

The final step is to sound out the alternatives. The best alternative to an agreement is sought. The question is what would happen if a deal fell through, what the damage would be and how things could continue without a deal. As a result, you should look elsewhere and be prepared for this eventuality. Look for several possible alternatives and decide for yourself which would be the best, in which case you no longer have to take the will of the other party into account.

This step is important for the Harvard concept in order to see where you stand. The idea is to evaluate how much an agreement is worth. Once you know how much worse off you would be without the deal, you have a framework. This gives you room to maneuver, as you can now discuss freely with your opponent within this framework.

The deal must be somewhere between your best case - the original interest - and the best alternative. If it is below this, you will fall back on your best alternative. This gives you a better idea of what you should risk for a deal. How much time, money and nerves is it worth sacrificing to reach an agreement? Is your best alternative only marginally worse than a possible agreement and are the negotiations very deadlocked? Consider an exit. Are you dependent on an agreement because the best alternative is worth nothing compared to an agreement? Approach the discussion with a willingness to compromise, lower your expectations and accommodate your counterpart. You will be given a tool that you can use to assess the necessary effort and adjust accordingly. The aim is therefore always to find an agreement that is better than the best alternative to an agreement.

You want to conclude a contract for your fruit stand for 100 kilograms of bananas per month. However, your contract partner has recently increased the price and is now charging €90 per 100 kilograms. Previously it was €70. He is not cooperating with regard to a possible joint profit solution. In your previous planning, you always had a budget of €80 for bananas per month. You would therefore have to negotiate your partner down to this €80. Look around for other suppliers first. What is their offer? Is it possible to negotiate with them? Also familiarize yourself with a complete elimination. What would it mean if you stopped selling bananas? Could you possibly use your budget elsewhere? What would that mean for your profit? Or is there no alternative to offering bananas in this case?

Would it perhaps even be worthwhile to sell off parts of your remaining range so that you can meet the demands of your contractual partner? All of this needs to be evaluated. Be clear about the importance of your interests in the conflict in general. How bad would it be to fall back on your best alternative?

At the same time, you should also bear in mind that stalled negotiations could cost you a considerable amount of money. In this specific case, you should consider that if you rely on your contractual partner, you could possibly miss a month's delivery due to ongoing disagreements. Let's say your best alternative would be to adjust the budget slightly and buy 100 kilograms of bananas for €85 from another supplier who is equally unwilling to negotiate.

It must then be clear to you that you must not miss the monthly delivery under any circumstances. So try to strike a deal with your original partner for between 70 and 85 euros without going over the monthly limit. This is then the framework within which you can operate. Let's look back at the five points of the Harvard concept before applying them comprehensively together in a final example. First of all, focus on the problem without projecting onto the person. Stay sober and don't get personal, it's about resolving a conflict, not changing a person. Next, focus on your interest and that of the other person. Leave out underlying positions and beliefs and focus your attention on the specific situation and the goals of both sides for the future.

Then look for possible ways to reconcile these interests. The best case scenario is that both parties are ultimately better off than before the conflict. To achieve this, look for different solutions, evaluate them and present them to your partner. In order to ensure a fair and measurable discourse, establish objective criteria after point four that can be used to assess the conflict, the interests and the solutions. These must be equally accessible and actually measurable for both parties. Finally, look outside the conflict for alternatives to an agreement and find the best one there. To do this, you should work out various options and select the best one. With this framework between interest and alternative, you can recognize the value of an agreement and thus weigh up how much you can accommodate the party involved in the conflict. Ultimately, you will reach an agreement this way.

Finally, this is applied to an example so that the whole process is brought a little closer to you. The case is explained very simply and quickly: you ask your boss for a pay rise. Previously you were earning €2,500 a month, but now you are asking for €3,000. Your boss thinks that you haven't been working there long enough and that a pay rise has to be earned long and hard. You, on the other hand, are of the opinion that you should have earned it long ago, as you have recently closed many deals and brought the company various new customers. The lack of appreciation bothers you and in your eyes it is time for your value to the company to be recognized and reflected financially. Your boss, however, tells you that you have primarily been lucky with your recent deals.

Apply step one. The problem here is that you're not getting the raise you want because your boss doesn't think you deserve it yet. That should be your focus in trying to resolve the conflict. It doesn't matter if you think he is ungrateful and finds his views outdated and slowing you down. That is not a factor in this conflict and it is not helpful. You must therefore meticulously focus on not getting personal right from the start. It's not about your boss, it's about a potential pay rise. Personal preferences should be left out of the equation, because as soon as you get personal, the basis for a discussion may already be broken. Your boss could now take any criticism personally, which would mean that emotions come into play, the parties are no longer objective and no solution can be reached. Accordingly, focus on the problem of the pay rise.

Continue with step two: Focus on interests instead of positions. To do this, first specify your interests. You want a pay rise. Your boss doesn't want that. He wants to save the money and keep a salary increase as something that has to be worked for. It is not relevant why he thinks this way and what basic attitude this interest is born of. Equally irrelevant is your own basic position on salary increases. It's all about this particular case and what you both want to gain from this conflict. In this scenario, it is therefore best to concentrate on the simple opposing interests: Salary increase versus refusal of the same.

At this point, you have now eliminated the main points of contention, removed a lot of emotionality from the conflict and taken important steps towards a healthy basis for discussion. After that, it's more about the content. You have defined your two interests in concrete terms, now you need to try to reconcile them. First look for a wide range of possible solutions. What would an agreement in the middle at around € 2,700 look like? Could something outside of this conventional solution also be an option?

What if you receive the €3,000, but sign a longer employment contract in return and thus, to a certain extent, meet your supervisor's requirement to work long hours? Is a slightly different job an option? Can you adjust your working hours? Perhaps a company car would be sufficient compensation? Are you perhaps even confident enough to make a kind of bet? For example, you could ask for the desired salary increase on the condition that you conclude 3 more deals in the remaining year. In general, there are no limits to your creativity. Anything is possible, so consider all these ideas and choose the best option for you. Involve your partner so that their interests are also taken into account. It is usually possible to find a situation that benefits both of you economically. It is important to find this. With the key of creativity and both interests in mind, this can be achieved quickly.

It is important to agree on criteria to help you evaluate these ideas, categorize the interests and determine what the overall conflict is about and what should play a role. These must be objective and accessible to both parties. Don't just say you've done a good job, put numbers to it. How many deals? How much turnover brought in? On the other hand, it is just as important to present your boss's interests in a measurable way. How long have you worked for the company? Have you ever had a pay rise? It is also useful to use precedents and comparisons in order to better assess the situation. What is the normal salary for an employee in your position in the company? After how many years is the average salary increase in this company? Once you have agreed on these criteria, it is easier to discuss on the same level, subjectivity is removed and ideas for solutions can be categorized more measurably according to their advantages for the parties.

Last but not least, look around for alternatives. Parallel to the search for a solution, it's all about creativity and a variety of options. Do you have other job offers? Are there comparable vacancies that pay better? Perhaps you should already apply to a few companies. Is your best alternative nonetheless to stay with the company and continue earning €2,500 a month? Weigh up these alternatives and choose the best one for you. Also consider time factors, for example whether you would have to go without a salary for a while if you changed jobs. Let's assume you have a job offer where you could earn €2,600 under otherwise similar circumstances. You now know that you should ask for at least €2,600. You have established criteria that you can use to better measure your value to the company. You have created a basis for discussion that is free of emotionality and heat. The only thing left to do is to try to outbid your best alternative. However, you also know that it is not worth continuing the discussion for months, as you have a good alternative. You have therefore fulfilled all the requirements and can resolve the conflict either by reaching an agreement or by withdrawing and changing companies.

What are the takeaways from the Harvard concept? The Harvard concept has a very sober approach, places particular emphasis on economic progress and is therefore also used in such fields. It shows you methods for eliminating emotionality and subjective views and then helps you to resolve the conflict using objective instruments. It also measures the value of this discussion and provides information on how much you should invest. Above all, you should remember to lay a basis for discussion, as this can also be beneficial outside of professional and business purposes. Leave people and positions out of it, think purposefully and try to ensure objectivity. The solution-oriented approach to the issue is positive in that it prevents you from getting caught up in current problems or past dislikes. The perspective is impersonal and rational.

If you see the concept in the context for which it is intended, it can help you to have a goal-oriented discourse more quickly and avoid fundamental discussions, disputes or disagreements based on subjective preferences. Once you have reached this point, the Harvard method can help you to seek developments and mutual profit. If possible, you should always create a negotiating framework, as this will enable you to avoid worthless and stalling conflicts more quickly. You should therefore always focus on a worst-case scenario and a best-case scenario. All in all, the creation of a basis for discussion and looking to the future should be kept in mind and applied more or less depending on the situation.

Of course, it is important to remember that the Harvard concept is intended for international legal disputes and the like and therefore does not always apply perfectly to other situations. If you're arguing with a relative over a point of principle, it's not necessarily going to be resolved by enlarging the pie. Although the Harvard concept may be helpful in such scenarios, it is important to see the model for what it is: an approach to economic progress. In doing so, it neglects social relationships, does not fully take into account how difficult objectivity can be in disputes in, say, a marriage, and does not emphasize sustaining sympathies and affections, only business relationships.

The fact that the sober approach and the often blunt and absolute evaluation process based on objective criteria can cause damage is also overlooked. If one spouse complains about the other's lack of effort, it is better not to use the money contributed, the number of times a week they vacuum or other marriages as a comparison.

Interpersonal relationships often require sensitivity and consideration. Another weakness of the method is that, although it paves the way for finding a solution, there will always be situations in which you cannot make progress even with the given tools and there seems to be no solution in sight. Even if the best alternative is found, there are conflicts in which the best alternative is not possible or is so significantly worse that it is practically impossible to avoid the conflict. To stay with the example of the married couple, divorce as the best alternative is so devastating for the lives of both of them that it is practically out of the question in a conflict, so in the vast majority of cases the conflict must be confronted.

The Harvard concept also relies to a large extent on creativity - note the process of finding solutions and the best alternatives. However, this is a gift that not everyone has and without which the concept often leaves you empty-handed. How can you solve the conflict without creative ways? In this case, few means are given to solve it.

The Harvard model leads the conflict leaders to a point from which solutions can be thought about and discussed, but does not offer any specific methods for finding and working them out. On the one hand, the search for a win-win situation is undoubtedly a good idea, but on the other hand this is not always easy and there is not always an optimal solution that benefits everyone involved. In these situations, it is difficult to make progress with the Harvard concept. In conclusion, it should be noted that the Harvard concept is not always applicable to every situation, that it neglects social aspects and interpersonal problems and therefore places less emphasis on the sustainable existence of such relationships, that it provides hardly any methodology with which solutions can actually be worked out and that it is largely based on creativity.

MEDIATION

As you can see, the Harvard method has its advantages and disadvantages, but you can learn something from it in any case. Nevertheless, it is certainly helpful to use a model that is more tailored to the everyday conflicts of life. One such method, which can be applied to all areas of life, is mediation. In mediation, a mediator is placed at the side of the conflicting parties, who guides and accompanies both parties on the path to finding a solution. The mediator is not concerned with content, but solely with the process, and is there to ensure a civilized and goal-oriented discourse. The Harvard concept is a form of such mediation which, as already mentioned, focuses on the business world.

There are also forms of mediation that are tailored to the family or school context. As the focus in these contexts is on personal relationships, more emphasis is placed on interpersonal aspects. This means that more emphasis is placed on the feelings of the other party and their views and character traits are taken into account. The mediator ensures this by allowing both parties the freedom to express and explain themselves at certain stages.

In this way, the empathy of the other party is addressed and both parties feel taken seriously and respected, so that the frustration threshold rises and emotions are taken away. You will not want to engage a mediator for every conflict, otherwise you would probably never have read this book. That is why the steps and procedures outlined below are also helpful without a mediator if you apply them yourself, and they will enable you to view the conflict from the perspective of a mediator and thus create the necessary space for both sides.

In the first step of mediation, basic discussion rules are established and a plan for the process is created. This serves as the basis for a suitable discourse and provides the parties with cornerstones within which they can act and hold back the opponents to the conflict. Furthermore, everyone knows what to expect and there are no unpleasant surprises.

Without a mediator, it may of course be somewhat more difficult to establish this, but it should be borne in mind that the rules here should be kept very basic. This means, for example, that the voice should not be raised, everyone should be allowed to speak and the other person's feelings should be respected. The same applies without a mediator: If your dispute partner does not agree to such conditions, you should not continue to discuss with them, but rather avoid them. However, as such guidelines are in the interests of all parties involved, there should hardly be anyone who disagrees with them.

Each side is then given time to present their points of contention, facts and concerns. Everyone can describe the conflict from their point of view, mention what specifically bothers them or what is particularly important to them. This makes it easier for everyone to put themselves in the other person's shoes, and the causes of the dispute become clear relatively quickly, as the greatest potential for conflict lies where there are particularly strong differences in viewpoints and perceptions. This is precisely where it is crucial that everyone is given free time to express themselves. This step is particularly important for mediation in schools. It may be difficult at times if the other person says something that you have perceived completely differently, but it is extremely important to allow them to disclose this. This makes them feel heard and respected, otherwise frustration increases.

In the third step, everything that can be found about a point of conflict in the dispute is collected: Facts, data, information and subjective feelings. The primary aim is to illuminate the conflict from all sides. Some methods of the Harvard concept are also applied here. For example, it is recommended to establish criteria and focus on interests. In this way, the main objectives of the parties should be worked out and, if possible, the underlying emotions. This is more difficult in the interpersonal field than in the economic field. This is because emotions in particular can often be hidden from all parties involved and tend to have a subconscious effect on the behavior of the person in question. By bringing everything surrounding the conflict to the surface and expressing it, the interests and feelings of the people involved can be clearly outlined. It also helps to eliminate misunderstandings. As a result, everyone knows where you and others stand and can work towards a solution.

In the penultimate step, solutions are collected. This is similar to the third step of the Harvard concept, but differs in that more emphasis is placed on exchange and ideas are thrown into the room, worked out and evaluated in open discourse. It is about cooperation, which should be made possible by the previous steps to bring the disputants closer together.

A mediator would always insist on consideration and ensure that both parties are equally satisfied with

the solution. This is undoubtedly more difficult without a mediator, but it is nonetheless possible thanks
to the previous steps if both sides are prepared to
present their ideas in an empathetic and respectful
manner. Ideas are presented, the other party can express themselves, based on which they can be modified
or discarded, and ideas that are not discarded are put
back to be compared with the other solutions until the
best option is determined.

Finally, the results are recorded. Depending on the
circumstances, this can be done in writing or verbally.
In the workplace, a written form is probably recommended, whereas in private life a verbal agreement
may be sufficient. It is crucial that the steps to be taken
and any obligations of the parties are recorded so that
the other party can claim these more easily and all sides are sure to agree on the same thing and no misunderstandings arise. A formal agreement is more likely
to oblige the parties to actually comply with it.

It is important to have a detailed and precise for-
mulation that leaves as little leeway as possible and
takes both sides equally into account. At this point,
there is no more negotiation, as the solution has already been worked out in step four, only the recording
of this solution is of importance here. Nevertheless, it

is advisable for both sides to be present so that nobody feels cheated or disadvantaged and everything has been thought of.

As you can see, there are certain similarities to the Harvard concept. The somewhat more time-consuming structure, which would probably not be implemented in purely economic circumstances, gives the participants more room for their interests and feelings. A positive aspect of this is that everyone feels respected, and especially if you have private or even family disputes, this simple trick can take a lot of antipathy out of the dispute.

The approach to finding a solution should also be emphasized positively. By soberly collecting all relevant information in the first step, the parties are on the same side and work together to resolve the conflict. After the second step, the disputants become even more familiar with each other's side, understanding is gained and consensus is sought. The approach of finding solutions through dialog and exchange rather than economic gain is more likely to ensure that both parties are satisfied personally and not just in terms of the objective end product. Finally, it is an advantage if you keep a written record of the outcome in mind, as this is also easier to implement.

On the other hand, there are also some disadvantages to mediation. The most important of these is probably the fact that a mediator is required for traditional mediation. Every step becomes a greater hurdle if it is carried out without a mediator. Therefore, what has just been described should rather be seen as an orientation or inspiration on how to conduct a more personal conflict in an orderly manner. Furthermore, this method is sometimes time-consuming and it can be nerve-wracking to listen to your counterpart's version of events, which you yourself do not agree with at all.

Similar to the Harvard concept, another problem is that the actual solution finding takes place without much guidance. Although finding a solution as a team is helpful, creativity is nevertheless required in a hopeless situation, without which it is impossible to move forward. Depending on the behavior of your counterpart, these hurdles may be smaller or almost insurmountable if he or she is resistant. Like all approaches, mediation should be seen in relative terms, as no approach to conflict resolution can avoid a completely uncooperative negotiating partner.

All in all, mediation therefore offers a helpful approach to conflict resolution in a more interpersonal context, but it should be viewed from a distance due to its shortcomings in places. Nevertheless, the approaches used to convey a sense of respect to the other party and the joint search for solutions based on empathy remain important.

Now that you have been given an insight into current approaches and research, you will have understood the complexity of the topic. There is simply no one universally correct way. This is the problem with simple step-by-step instructions: They are either too open and vague or they are so specific that the most important step first is to recognize whether you can apply them at all.

Therefore, the key thing you can take away from this book is the values and ways of thinking that the approaches use. For example, you can apply empathy, objectivity in assessment - using criteria, for example - or sober consideration and consideration of the options given to you as instruments in problem situations. To illustrate this, the following section provides you with a rough guide that you can fall back on in cases of conflict and that you can apply freely and structurally detached or close to the original structure. The aim here is not so much to create a set of instructions that you can use blindly to resolve every dispute, but rather to be able to classify the conflict and then resolve it using the tools you have learned about.

For this reason, it is also crucial to internalize them and be able to apply them accordingly, because no instructions in the world can automatically resolve a dispute. However, this will not be difficult once you have familiarized yourself with the subject matter and taken some time to get to know it, so that routine and level-headedness will soon set in.

Put simply, this orientation should help you to make the best of the conflict. That would of course be to achieve your interests and restore harmony between the parties. The initial aim is to achieve as much of both aspects as possible. However, there will always be situations in which absolute harmony and achieving all your interests are not completely compatible. This guide will first help you to make your conflict partner as cooperative as possible so that you can then weigh up the two aspects and decide how and to what extent your interests should be weighted.

Finally, you will be supported in your further course of action so that you can decide more soberly what the best option is - to discuss to the end, to accommodate, to avoid the conflict and look elsewhere or similar. The origins of conflicts are addressed and the methods explained are also incorporated so that the process is as practical, broadly applicable and balanced as possible. It should be noted at this point that success always depends on external factors and, above all, your counterpart, but you will never go wrong with this method or make the situation worse. It merely serves to achieve the best possible result - what this is depends on the specific case.

So how do you act in a conflict situation? There is a disagreement between you and another person from which a dispute could arise or has already arisen. You want to resolve this. First and foremost, put your emotions, interests and goals second and focus on the conversation. It doesn't matter what was said, what the issue is or who you are talking to. Your top priority now is to establish a healthy culture of conversation that you can then build on. This is your first pillar of orientation: creating a basis for conversation. No matter what the situation looks like, you will never be at a disadvantage because you take care of one. Even if you are wrong and there is no conflict at all, this step will not ruin anything.

In order to establish this basis for discussion, you must first de-escalate the situation. This step will sometimes cost you the most effort if you and the other party to the conflict have already had a serious clash and emotions are involved. Remember, emotions are the main cause of disputes, so it is also important to remove them from the conversation. So jump over your shadow and accommodate your counterpart. Similar to mediation, give them space to express themselves and explain their views. Listen to them, don't interrupt them and give them the feeling that they are respected and heard. You may be reluctant to do this at first, but it will also benefit you in the long run. Afterwards, you can also demand to be heard briefly.

The likelihood that the other person will actually listen to you increases enormously if you have taken the first step and given them the benefit of the doubt. This first step takes a lot of the sharpness and volume out of the conversation and can possibly clarify initial questions or misunderstandings; both parties meet respectfully and at eye level.

Of course, you don't have to interrupt the conversation and give the other person their five-minute plea. You can also enforce this basic respect more subtly by starting to listen to them more attentively and letting them feel it. You will notice that in most cases your counterpart will automatically replicate this behavior. If he doesn't, it can also help to draw his attention to this and ask him to change it, because you are also letting him finish and treating him with respect.

Another prerequisite for the basis of the conversation is empathy. Although this will not immediately soften the mood of the person you are arguing with, it will help you to keep a cool head and avoid unnecessary differences of opinion in the conflict. Ask yourself whether they could be right on some points, whether they have positive motives and intentions or whether you can at least understand them. Conflicts often arise from the same intentions of two people, which are then opposed. The simplest example of this is when two people want the same thing.

On the other hand, it is also possible that two people benefit from the same case but do not recognize this due to a lack of empathy. In both cases, putting yourself in the other person's shoes removes aversions and creates connections. It seems less like you are both adversaries and more like you are partners in the same predicament. It can also lead to your partner picking up on your behavior, as with attentive listening, and also trying to understand your situation. In any case, differences are bridged. As you will notice, however, the first orientation pillar requires a certain amount of courage on your part, as you usually have to take the first step. If you find this particularly difficult, keep reminding yourself that you are doing this for yourself and will benefit from it. Again, there is no need to follow a strict pattern. It is just helpful to keep in mind the question of whether you can understand the other person.

In the final step towards a healthy and productive basis for discussion, empathy is strengthened even further and an attempt is made to find common ground from which the rest can be clarified. Think of it as initially leaving everything that is excess behind. The aim is to prevent you from getting into an argument about a specific topic in fundamental debates in which you may disagree.

At the same time, the core of the thematic differences is found. This can be achieved by asking your discussion partner whether you at least agree on completely fundamental issues. This narrows the circle of conflict and avoids unnecessary discussions. In addition, you continue to come closer together and can argue from this common viewpoint and clarify the differences. While you were still questioning and reining yourself in during the empathy step, you are now clarifying in open discourse what you agree on, what the core of the conflict is and which discussions are superfluous. You can bring this up, for example, if you have the feeling that the other person is trying to convince you of something that you already believe or if they are getting lost in an obviousness and thus dragging the discussion on.

A quick question or affirmation can create common ground. However, make sure you do this respectfully, otherwise she may take it as an insult. Here you can also establish common criteria according to the Harvard method and thus argue more objectively. This removes another source of contention with a person's subjective point of view and brings the parties closer together. This ensures a healthy basis for a goal-oriented discussion.

The second central pillar of orientation is classifying the conflict. By reflecting on what is important to you, you can make better decisions about how to proceed. This involves clarifying what you hope to gain from the conflict, what there is to lose and how you feel about the other party. Central to this point is the question of how you weight which interests. Often the parties involved are not fully aware of what is at stake, so it is helpful to be clear about this. This is the only way you can then weigh up the risks and plan the outcome of the conflict accordingly.

In order to achieve this, you must first consider all your interests. Reflect on the original goal with which you entered the conflict. Other goals may have emerged during the conflict, but you should ask your-self whether these have arisen in the heat of the moment.

It is therefore important to always differentiate between objectively useful interests, which are beneficial in the long term, and subjective goals, which are more about being right, getting even or dislikes. So take a calm and focused look at your goals and weigh up what is really important to you. At this point, you can also select or prioritize. However, this step is initially limited to factual, substantive interests. It can also happen that you realize that your actual interest is no longer achievable due to the conflict or that it has been completely resolved. In order to avoid unnecessary disputes in such situations, it helps to focus on these interests.

On the other hand, there is your relationship with the other disputant. What does this mean to you, what kind of relationship do you have and what would a deterioration of this relationship mean for you? You should be particularly careful with relationships of dependency and keep this in mind at all times, otherwise precarious situations can quickly arise. Caution should also be exercised in the case of particularly personal or intimate relationships, as these are often accompanied, at least indirectly, by emotional dependency.

It should also be noted that the extent of a deteriorated relationship with the other person is often not apparent at first glance. Therefore, a complete break-up should always be avoided at all costs, as you never know how this could backfire on you. Be aware of all the possible and recognizable consequences of a broken relationship and always keep an even greater extent in mind.

The next step is to compare and weigh up the relationship with the conflict partner and your own interest in the conflict. How important are these and what should you therefore place more emphasis on? There is no need to make an absolute decision in the sense that either one or the other should be dropped. Rather, a balance is crucial. So in case of doubt, what would be more important and where are you prepared to cut back more and further?

The aim is to gain a better picture of what is actually at stake and to be able to make a better decision on how to proceed based on this. It often quickly becomes clear that the conflict is not worth jeopardizing the relationship, or that there is no alternative to your interest and no consideration can be given to the relationship.

However, don't be too hasty with final decisions and try to find the best solution on both sides afterwards. This also gives you leeway in terms of how far you can insist on the interest without seriously damaging the relationship and how far you can maintain harmony without abandoning your principles and damaging yourself. Ideally, you will be able to identify a turning point at which both sides will gain the most. For example, you will realize that you will benefit most if you reduce your interest by half and thus only marginally damage the relationship. If you continue to neglect your interest, it is no longer worth it and the relationship is hardly any better as a result, so this would be a worse solution. However, if you insist more on your interest, the relationship will suffer greater damage and negative consequences will arise, which would also be a worse solution. It is important to look for this golden point.

Finally, the third and last orientation pillar benefits from the created basis for discussion and implements what has been learned about the conflict with a view to the future. This pillar is intended to help find the best solution and thus form a productive and conciliatory end to the conflict. To this end, the objective and future-oriented way of thinking of the Harvard concept is used, and more personal aspects and the relationship with the conflict partner are also included. Material and immaterial costs are taken into account, so that the end result is a balanced and comprehensively illuminated situation for the disputing party, from which they can then resolve the dispute in the best possible way according to their possibilities.

The first step is to get an idea of the available options. To do this, the best alternatives are considered in line with the Harvard method in order to form a framework for negotiations. Include external options as well as those within the scope of the conflict. You should always have at least one alternative for each scenario. What is your best course of action if you have to avoid the conflict without achieving your interests?

What is your best course of action if you assert your interest in such a way that all bridges to the other party are torn down? As it will not always be possible to reach the golden point mentioned above, these alternatives help to set a scale on the side of interest. This allows you to look for the best alternative to your desired solution and to reach an agreement in the first place. The creativity requirement, which is viewed rather critically in the previous methods, is not necessarily present in this concept, as you can better orientate yourself to your conflict classification and consideration, which then puts missing alternatives in relation to the relationship in the absence of creativity, so that you can draw immediate conclusions. Nevertheless, a certain degree of creativity is undoubtedly an advantage here too and can sometimes provide a loophole.

Probably the best and simplest approach for finding other options is to search freely for every possibility and, as a first step, record everything that comes to mind. You can then make a selection and decide on the best alternative. It is particularly difficult to find the best alternative in conflicts where the emotional dependency on the conflict partner is very high.

At this point, there are two possibilities: Either you simply see no way out and you strongly prioritize the personal relationship over your interests or you find something within the conflict. This means that, similar to the Harvard concept, you find a way of enlarging the cake so that both sides are happy outside the conflict. In this way, it may be possible to preserve the relationship without settling the conflict if you can make peace elsewhere and overlook the differences in this specific area.

Once you have decided on your best alternative and found the framework for the negotiation or discussion, you need to consider the time it will take. What do you lose if the conflict drags on? Is the relationship steadily deteriorating, are you missing out on profits, are you missing an appointment? If you are under such time pressure, you must be aware that you are on the short end of the stick and may have to lower your standards further.

It is important to know whether your counterpart is aware of this time pressure. If he does, the only sensible thing to do is to be open and fair from the outset and make lower demands. If he doesn't know this, it may be worth taking the risk, but this should be weighed up soberly and carefully. So first make it clear what a longer negotiation means for you, whether the possible deterioration is on the relationship side or the interest side, and then take the other person's knowledge into account. Once you have done this, you can add this risk to your consideration of preserving the relationship and achieving your interests and are therefore ideally positioned for any negotiation scenario.

In this way, you can finally discuss the conflict. When doing so, balance your relationship and your interests and make sure that you keep the ratio of damage to both as previously weighed up. If you notice that the relationship is deteriorating to such an extent that you would be at a greater disadvantage than if you backed down with your interests, adjust your approach accordingly. The result at interest level should never fall short of your best alternative, otherwise you can simply give up the conflict, stop straining the relationship and pursue your alternative. This is often a matter of tact and, once again, empathy is a key virtue, as this is the only way you can assess the situation at relationship level.

Remain calm, continue to use methods to maintain the climate of the conversation and reflect on your considerations and your best alternative. This will help you to resolve the conflict so that both parties are happy. A final example can be used to illustrate what you have learned and clarify any questions you may have. Put yourself in the following scenario: You and a friend are big pizza fanatics. When the last pizzeria in your town closes, you both decide to open a pizzeria yourselves.

The planning is going well, but a conflict arises when it comes to deciding which oven to buy. You are firmly convinced that the necessary quality can only be achieved with a stone oven for around €5,000, while your colleague prefers a cheaper version for around half the price, because you can't taste the difference.

Now create a basis for discussion. You are both passionate about the project. Put this aside for the time being. Whether you think it is disgraceful to traditional pizza culture to use a metal oven and whether you are disappointed with your friend's attitude is irrelevant and should be put aside.

Give them the space to articulate themselves and their reasons. Pay attention to the volume and make sure you let him finish. Among friends, you can then ask him to listen to you, just as you did before. Make sure you listen empathetically to his explanation and consciously try to understand him. You share the same passion, so take his emotionality into account and remain understanding. You will realize that you both have the same drive and are acting out of similar situations. These similarities should now be emphasized. You both love pizza and both like a similar type of pizza. Their only point of contention is the nature of the oven. Discussions about the tradition of pizza making or anything similar are out of place. So make it clear to him and yourself that you are in the same boat, share the same interests and are both pursuing the goal of a good and successful pizzeria.

You can now have a calm and cultured conversation with your partner. Concentrate on yourself and on what the conflict is about. You are interested in an Italian-style pizzeria that is as tasty and profitable as possible. To achieve this, you want a stone oven. In the end, however, this is more of a means to an end. On the other hand, your friend is important to you and the friendship with shared passion is the origin of the project and therefore also the prerequisite for the pizzeria. Weigh things up. The relationship with your friend is more important here, the interest is clearly secondary. How exactly is this relationship structured? If you insist on your interest, you will easily jeopardize the friendship, which would be a loss for the business and for you privately. If you neglect your interest, the friendship will remain intact, with the only loss being a slightly better tasting pizza. Whether there is anything in between depends on alternative ovens, for example. Is there a center point where the overall gain - i.e. interest and relationship together - is higher in the end? This is your golden point that you should aim for in negotiations. If there isn't, you are best off neglecting your interests.

At this point, you need to look to the future and prepare for a goal-oriented negotiation. First look for alternatives on the interest side. In this case, this can be done quickly.

If you can't agree on the oven, your only option is to open the pizzeria on your own or scrap the idea. You could open a restaurant without a pizza oven, but then your passion for pizza would not be included and the only reason why you wanted to open a restaurant in the first place would disappear. Probably the best alternative would be to open nothing, as the costs alone would be harder to bear and the other options would remove either the friendship or the passion. The costs of a lengthy negotiation would not be significant in this case, as there are no deadlines to meet. What is your next course of action? There is more or less no alternative to an agreement; the relationship is strongly preferred. Of course, your friend is in the same situation, so you can negotiate. But stay calm and don't allow the conflict to cause more damage than a metal furnace. You may be generally satisfied with this outcome, but it may still be worth discussing it with your friend. This should always remain within the bounds of a healthy basis for discussion.

This means you are well prepared for a conflict of any kind. You won't always achieve your desired outcome, but you will achieve the best possible one under all circumstances. Hopefully you will have taken something away with you and feel well prepared for future disputes, because it is not a bad thing to get into them. You will be surprised how often you can apply what you have learned in everyday life.

www.ingramcontent.com/pod-product-compliance
Lightning Source LLC
Chambersburg PA
CBHW020120180726
47992CB00019B/1309